Knit
Stitch Guide
by Rita Weiss

CONTENTS

Leisure Arts, Inc.

Little Rock, Arkansas

PRODUCED BY

PRODUCTION TEAM

Creative Directors:	Jean Leinhauser and Rita Weiss
Technical Editor:	Ellen W. Liberles
Photographer:	Carol Wilson Mansfield
Pattern Tester:	Kimberly Britt
Book Design:	Linda Causee

PUBLISHED BY

© 2013 by Leisure Arts, Inc.,

5701 Ranch Drive,

Little Rock, AR 72223,

www.leisurearts.com.

Library of Congress Control Number: 2012954588
ISBN-13: 978-1-4647-0742-1

Introduction

Collecting and experimenting with interesting knitting stitches has always fascinated me. More than that, I especially enjoy sharing those stitches with other knitters in the books I have done filled with photos and instructions.

This book, however, is my favorite because of its small, compact size. Carry it with you along with your yarn, your needles and your tools wherever you may travel. Inside you'll find over 90 stitches that will add that extra something to your knitting pursuits.

What you won't find in this book is any mention of gauge. That's because you can work these stitches with any type or size of yarn—from a bulky weight to the finest lace weight. The photographed models in this book were actually made with Red Heart® Luster Sheen®, which is a size 2, fine weight yarn. The project you choose may look quite different depending upon the yarn you might choose for your particular project.

What you will find here is the word "multiple" at the start of each pattern. A multiple is the number of stitches needed to work one complete unit of the pattern. If the pattern says "Multiple: 6 + 4", you will need to cast on any number of stitches which can be evenly divided by 6: 12, 18, 24, or 30 for example. To this you will need to add the "+4" so you will cast on 4 more stitches to the total, giving—for example—16, 22, 28, or 34 stitches. Always remember that the plus (+) number is added only once.

So pick your favorite stitches and have fun swatching. You may discover—as I have—that the most difficult part of the job could very well be deciding which stitch is the one you want to use in your next project.

MOSS STITCH

Multiple: 2 + 2

Instructions

Row 1 (right side): K1; *K1, P1; rep from * to last st, K1.

Row 2: K1; *P1, K1; rep from * to last st, K1.

Repeat Rows 1 and 2 for pattern.

ANDALUSIAN STITCH

Multiple: 2 + 2

Instructions

Row 1 (right side): Knit across.

Row 2: K1; purl to last st, K1.

Row 3: K1; *K1, P1; rep from * to last st, K1.

Row 4: K1; purl to last st, K1.

ROMAN STITCH

Multiple: Any even number

Instructions

Row 1 (right side): Knit across.

Row 2: K1, purl to last st, K1.

Row 3: Knit.

Row 4: K1, purl to last st, K1.

Row 5: K1; *K1, P1; rep from * to last st, K1.

Row 6: K1; *P1, K1; rep from * to last st, K1.

Repeat Rows 1 through 6 for pattern, ending by working Row 4.

MOIRE STITCH

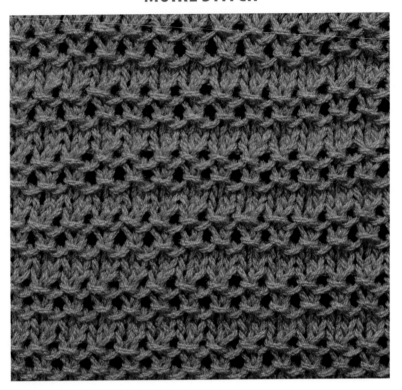

Multiple: 2 + 2

STITCH GUIDE

wyif: with yarn in front

wyib: with yarn in back

PSKYO: pass slip stitch over knit stitch and YO

Instructions ────────

Row 1 (right side): K1; * wyif sl 1 as if to purl, wyib K1, YO, PSKYO; rep from * to last st, K1.

Row 2: K1, purl to last st, K1.

Row 3: Rep Row 1.

Row 4: K1; purl to last st, K1.

Row 5: Knit.

Row 6: K1; purl to last st, K1.

Repeat Rows 1 through 6 for pattern.

───────────────

IRISH MOSS STITCH

Multiple 4 + 2

Instructions ——————

Row 1: K1; *K1, P1; rep from * to last st, K1.

Row 2: K1; *P1, K1; rep from * to last st, K1.

Row 3: K1; *P1, K1; rep from * to last st, K1.

Row 4: K1; *K1, P1; rep from * across to last st, K1.

Repeat Rows 1 through 4 for pattern.

LINEN STITCH

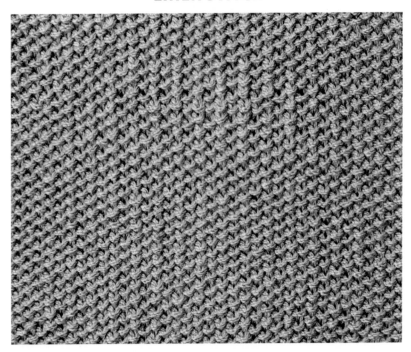

Multiple: 2 + 2

STITCH GUIDE

wyif: with yarn in front

wyib: with yarn in back

Instructions

Row 1: K1, *K1, wyif, sl 1 as if to purl, wyib; rep from * to last st, K1.

Row 2 (right side): K1; *P1, wyib sl 1 as if to purl, wyif; rep from * to last st, K1.

Repeat Rows 1 and 2 for pattern.

TWEED STITCH

Multiple: 2 + 2

Instructions

Row 1 (right side): K1; *K1, wyif, sl 1 as to purl, wyib; rep from * to last st, K1.

Row 2: K1, purl to last st, K1.

Row 3: K1; *wyif, sl 1 as to purl, wyib, K1; rep from * to last st, K1.

Row 4: K1, purl to last st, K1.

Repeat Rows 1 through 4 for pattern.

SWAG STITCH

Multiple: 5 + 4

Instructions ──────────

Row 1 (wrong side): K1; purl to last st, K1.

Row 2 (right side): Knit.

Row 3: K1; purl to last st, K1.

Row 4: K1, P2; *wyif sl 3, P2; rep from * to last st, K1.

Row 5: K1; purl to last st, K1.

Row 6: K1, P2; *wyif sl 3, P2; rep from * to last st, K1.

Repeat Rows 1 through 6 for pattern, ending by working Row 1.

TWISTED TIE

Mutiple: 2 + 2

Instructions ───────

Row 1 (right side): Knit.

Row 2: K1, K2tog across to last st, K1.

Row 3: K1, Knit into front and back of each st to last st, K1.

Row 4: K1, purl to last st, K1.

Repeat Rows 1 through 4 for pattern.

ZIG ZAG

Multiple: 10 + 2

Instructions

Row 1 (right side): K1; *K5, (P1, K1) twice, P1; rep from * across to last st, K1.

Row 2: K1; *(P1, K1) 3 times, P4; rep from * across to last st, K1.

Row 3: K1; *K3, (P1, K1) twice, P1, K2; rep from * to last st, K1.

Row 4: K1; *P3, (K1, P1) twice, K1, P2; rep from * to last st, K1.

Row 5: K1; *(K1, P1) 3 times, K4; rep from * to last st, K1.

Row 6: K1; *P5, (K1, P1) twice, K1; rep from * to last st, K1.

Row 7: K1; *(K1, P1) 3 times, K4; rep from * to last st, K1.

Row 8: K1; *P3, (K1, P1) twice, K1, P2; rep from * to last st, K1.

Row 9: K1; *K3, (P1, K1) twice, P1, K2; rep from * across, ending last rep with K3.

Row 10: K1; *(P1, K1) 3 times, P4; rep from * across, to last st, K1.

Repeat Rows 1 through 10 for pattern.

BASKETWEAVE

Multiple: 8 + 3

Instructions

Row 1 (wrong side): Purl.

Row 2: K3; *P5, K3; rep from * across.

Row 3: P3; *K5, P3; rep from * across.

Row 4: K3; *P5, K3; rep from * across.

Row 5: Purl.

Row 6: P4; *K3, P5; rep from * across, ending last rep with P4.

Row 7: K4; *P3, K5; rep from * across, ending last rep with K4.

Row 8: P4; *K3, P5; rep from * across, ending last rep with P4.

Repeat Rows 1 through 8 for pattern.

WOVEN LATTICE

Multiple: 14 + 12

Instructions ——————

Row 1 (wrong side): Purl across.

Row 2, 4, 6, 8, 12, 14, 16, 18: (P1, K1) twice, P1; *K2, (P1, K1) twice, P1; rep from * across.

Rows 3, 5, 7, 13, 15 and 17: (P1, K1) twice; *P4, K1, P1, K1; rep from * across, ending with P1.

Row 9: K5; *P2, K12; rep from *, ending last rep with P2, K5.

Row 10: P5; *K2, P12; rep from * ending last rep with K2, P5.

Row 11: Purl across.

Row 19: K5; *P2, K12; rep from *, ending last rep with P2, K5.

Row 20: P5; *K2, P12; rep from * across, ending last rep with K2, P5.

Repeat Rows 1 through 20 for pattern.

OPTICAL ILLUSION

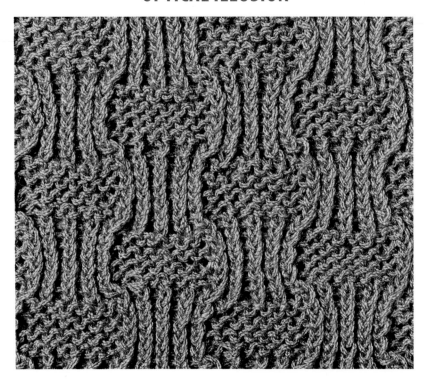

Multiple: 16 + 1

Instructions

Row 1 (right side): *(K1tbl, P1) 4 times, K1tbl, P7; rep from * across, ending with K1.

Rows 2, 4, 6 and 8: P1; *P7, (P1tbl, K1) 4 times, P1tbl; rep from * across.

Rows 3, 5 and 7: *(K1tbl, P1) 4 times, K1tbl, P7; rep from * across, ending with K1.

Rows 9, 11, 13 and 15: K1; *P7, (K1tbl, P1) 4 times, K1tbl; rep from * across.

Rows 10, 12, 14 and 16: *(P1tbl, K1) 4 times, P1tbl, P7; rep from * across, ending with P1.

Repeat Rows 1 through 16 for pattern.

GARTER STITCH DIAMONDS

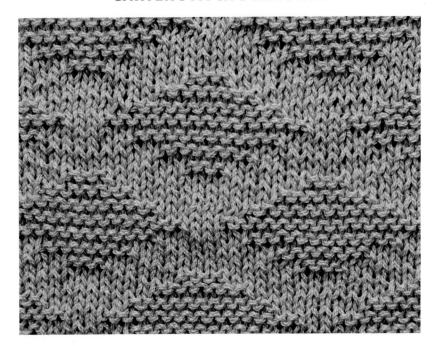

Multiple: 18 + 1

Instructions

Row 1 (right side): Knit across.

Row 2: K2; *P6, K3; rep from * across, ending last rep with K2.

Row 3 and all odd rows: Knit.

Rows 4 and 12: P6; *K7, P11; rep from * across, ending last rep with P6.

Rows 6 and 10: P4; *K11, P7; rep from * across, ending last rep with P4.

Row 8: P2; *K15, P3; rep from * across, ending last rep with P2.

Row 14: K2; *P6, K3; rep from * across, ending last rep with K2.

Row 16: K4; *P11, K7; rep from * across, ending last rep with K4.

Row 18 and 22: K6; *P7, K11; rep from * across, ending last rep with K6.

Row 20: K8; *P3, K15; rep from * across, ending last rep with K8.

Row 24: K4; *P11, K7; rep from * across, ending last rep with K4.

Repeat Rows 1 through 24 for pattern.

WIDE BASKET STITCH

Multiple: 9 + 8

Instructions ————

Row 1 (right side): K1; *P6, K3; rep from * to last 7 sts, P6, K1.

Row 2: K1; *K6, P3; rep from * to last 7 sts, K7.

Row 3: Rep Row 1.

Row 4: Rep Row 2.

Row 5: K1; *P6, K3; rep from * to last 7 sts, P6, K1.

Row 6: Rep Row 2.

Row 7: Rep Row 2.

Row 8: Rep Row 1.

Row 9: Rep Row 2.

Row 10: Rep Row 1.

Repeat Rows 1 through 10 for pattern

GRANITE RIDGE

Multiple: 2

Instructions

Row 1 (right side): Knit across.

Row 2: K1, purl across to last st, K1.

Row 3: Knit across.

Row 4: K1, purl across to last st, K1.

Row 5: Knit across.

Row 6: K1; K2tog across row to last st, K1.

Row 7: K1; *(K1, P1) into st; rep from * across to last st, K1.

Row 8: K1, purl across to last st, K1.

Repeat Rows 1 through 8 for pattern.

FLYING GEESE

Multiple: 12 + 2

Instructions

Row 1 (right side): K1; *K6, P1, K5; rep from * to last st, K1.

Row 2: K1; *P4, K3, P5; rep from * to last st, K1.

Row 3: K1; *K4, P5, K3; rep from * to last st, K1.

Row 4: K1; *P2, K7, P3; rep from * to last st, K1.

Row 5: K1; *K2, P9, K1; rep from * to last st, K1.

Row 6: K1, purl to last st, K1.

Row 7: K1; *P1, K11; rep from * to last st, K1

Row 8: K1; *K1, P9, K2; rep from * to last st, K1.

Row 9: K1; *P3, K7, P2; rep from * to last st, K1.

Row 10: K1; *K3, P5, K4; rep from * to last st, K1.

Row 11: K1; *P5, K3, P4; rep from * to last st, K1.

Row 12: K1, purl to last st, K1.

Repeat Rows 1 through 12 for pattern.

DIAGONAL TWEED

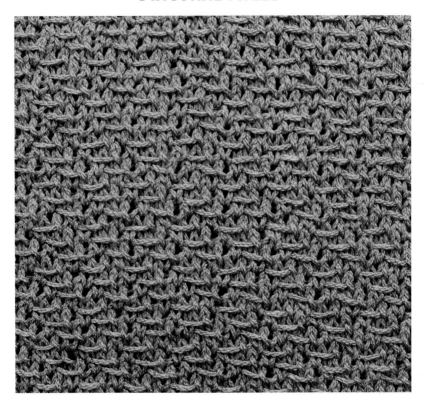

Multiple: 4

Instructions

Row 1 (right side): K1; *K2, wyif sl 2, wyib; rep from * to last 3 sts, K3.

Row 2: K1, purl to last st, K1.

Row 3: K1, wyif sl 1, wyib; *K2, wyif sl 2, wyib; rep from * to last 2 sts, K2.

Row 4: K1, purl to last st, K1.

Row 5: K1, wyif sl 2, wyib ; *K2, wyif sl 2, wyib; rep from * across to last st, K1.

Row 6: K1, purl to last st, K1.

Repeat Rows 1 through 6 for pattern.

STAMEN STITCH

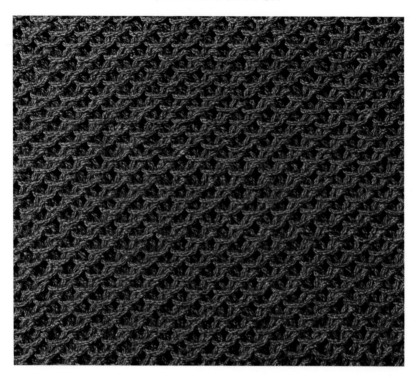

Multiple: 2

Note: *Work this stitch with large needles. Slip stitches as if to purl.*

Instructions ───────

Row 1 (right side): Knit across.

Row 2: *K1, sl 1, rep from * across, ending with K2.

Row 3: Knit across.

Row 4: K2; *sl 1, K1; rep from * across.

Repeat Rows 1 through 4 for pattern.

SIMPLE BRIOCHE STITCH

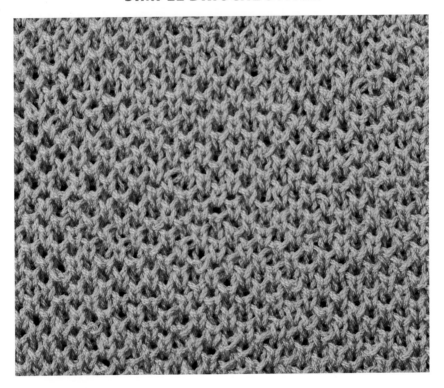

Multiple: any even number

STITCH GUIDE:

K1B (Knit 1 below): Insert needle into stitch below next stitch on left-hand needle and knit it, slipping the stitch above off the needle at the same time: K1B made.

Instructions

Row 1: Knit across.

Row 2 (right side): K1; *K1, K1B; rep from * to last st, K1.

Row 3: Knit across.

Row 4: K1; *K1B, K1; rep from * to last st, K1.

Repeat Rows 1 through 4 for pattern.

SIMPLE RIB

Multiple: 4 sts

STITCH GUIDE

SSK (slip, slip, knit): Slip next two sts as if to knit, one at a time, to right-hand needle. Insert left needle into fronts of these stitches from left to right, and knit them together.

Instructions

Rows 1 through 3: *K2, P2; rep from * across.

Row 4 (right side): *SSK, YO, P2; rep from * across.

Row 5: *K2, P2; rep from * across.

Row 6: *YO, K2tog, P2; rep from * across.

Row 7: *K2, P2; rep from * across.

Row 8: *SSK, YO, P2; rep from * across.

Row 9: *K2, P2; rep from * across.

Row 10: *YO, K2tog, P2; rep from * across.

Rows 11 through 13: *K2, P2; rep from * across.

Repeat Rows 4 through 13 for pattern.

SIMPLE CABLE RIB

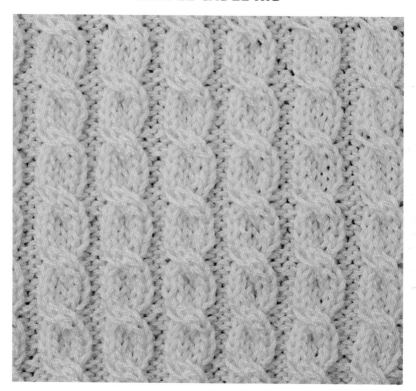

Multiple: 7+ 3

Note: *This pattern uses a cable needle (cn).*

Instructions

Row 1 (right side): *P3, K4; rep from *, ending with P3.

Row 2: *K3, P4; rep from * ending with K3

Row 3: Rep Row 1.

Row 4: Rep Row 2.

Row 5: *P3, sl 2 sts to cn and hold at front, K2, K2 from cn; rep from * across ending with P3.

Row 6: Rep Row 2.

Repeat Rows 1 through 6 for pattern.

LACE RIB

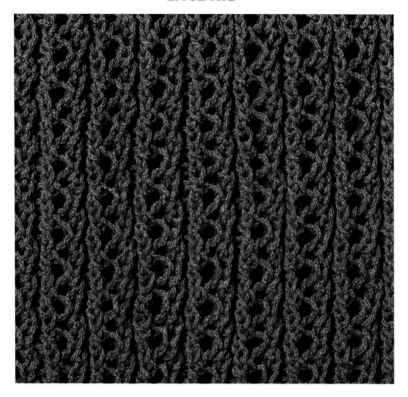

Multiple: 5 + 2

STITCH GUIDE

SSK (slip, slip, knit): Slip next two sts as if to knit, one at a time to right-hand needle. Insert left needle into fronts of these stitches from left to right, and knit them together.

Instructions

Row 1 (right side): P2; *K1, YO, SSK, P2; rep from * across.

Row 2: *K2, P3; rep from * to last 2 sts, K2.

Row 3: P2; *K2tog, YO, K1, P2; rep from * across.

Row 4: Rep Row 2.

Repeat Rows 1 to 4 for pattern.

SAILOR'S RIB

Multiple: 5 + 1

Instructions

Row 1 (right side): K1tbl, *P1, K2, P1, K1tbl; rep from * across.

Row 2: P1; *K1, P2, K1, P1; rep from * across.

Row 3: K1tbl; *P4, K1tbl; rep from * across.

Row 4: P1; *K4, P1; rep from * across.

Repeat Rows 1 through 4 for pattern.

TRAVELING RIB

Multiple: 6

Note: *Uses a cable needle (cn).*

Instructions

Row 1: *P2, T2L, K2; rep from * across.

Row 2: *P4, K2; rep from * across.

Row 3: *P2, K1, T2L, K1; rep from * across.

Row 4: Rep Row 2.

Row 5: *P2, K2, T2L; rep from * across.

Row 6: Rep Row 2.

Repeat Rows 1 through 6 for pattern.

SEEDED RIB CHECK

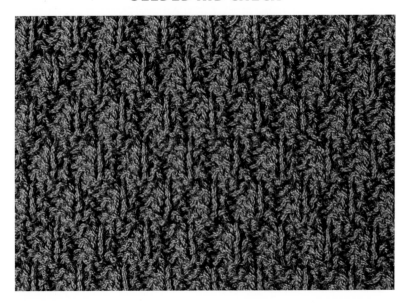

Multiple: 4 + 3

Instructions

Row 1 (right side): K3; *P1, K3; rep from * across.

Row 2: K1; *P1, K3; rep from * ending with P1, K1.

Rows 3: K3; *P1, K3; rep from * across.

Rows 4: K1; *P1, K3; rep from * ending with P1, K1.

Row 5: K3; *P1, K3; rep from * across

Row 6: K1; *P1, K3; rep from * ending with P1, K1.

Rows 7: K1; *P1, K3; rep from * ending with P1, K1.

Row 8: K3; *P1, K3; rep from * across.

Row 9: K1; *P1, K3; rep from * ending with P1, K1.

Row 10: K3; *P1, K3; rep from * across.

Row 11: K1; *P1, K3; rep from * ending with P1, K1.

Row 12: K3; *P1, K3; rep from * across.

Repeat Rows 1 through 12.

DIAGONAL RIB

Multiple: 6

Instructions ───────

Row 1 (right side): *P3, K3; rep from * across.

Row 2: *P3, K3; rep from * across.

Row 3: P2; *K3, P3; rep from * across, ending with K3, P1.

Row 4: K1, P3; *K3, P3; rep from * across, ending with K2.

Row 5: P1; *K3, P3; rep from * across, ending with K3, P2.

Row 6: K2, P3; *K3, P3; rep from * across, ending with K1.

Row 7: *K3, P3; rep from * across.

Row 8: *K3, P3; rep from * across.

Row 9: K2; *P3, K3; rep from * across to last 4 sts, P3, K1.

Row 10: P1, K3; *P3, K3; rep from * across, ending with P2.

Row 11: K1; *P3, K3; rep from * across, ending with P3, K2.

Row 12: P2, K3; *P3, K3; rep from * across, ending with P1.

Repeat Rows 1 to 12 for pattern.

SHELL RIB

Multiple: 5 + 2

Instructions ───────

Row 1 (right side): P2; *K3, P2; rep from * across.

Row 2: K2; *P3, K2; rep from * across.

Row 3: P2; *sl 1, K2tog, PSSO, P2; rep from * across.

Row 4: K2; *(P1, K1, P1 in next st), K2; rep from * across.

Repeat Rows 1 through 4 for pattern.

───────

EYELET RIB

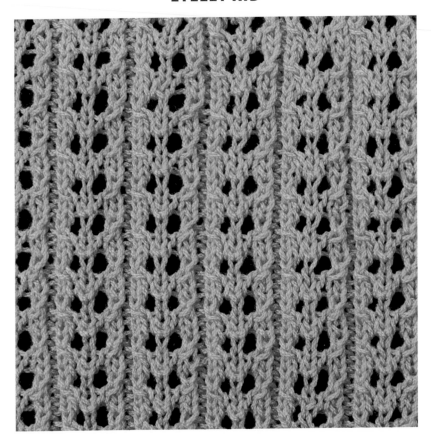

Multiple: 7 + 2

Instructions

Row 1: K2; *P5, K2; rep from * across.

Row 2 (right side): P2; *K5, P2; rep from * across.

Row 3: K2; *P5, K2; rep from * across.

Row 4: P2; *K2tog, YO, K1, YO, SSK, P2; rep from * across.

Repeat Rows 1 through 4 for pattern.

WHEAT EAR RIB

Multiple: 5 + 2

Note: *Uses a cable needle (cn)*

STITCH GUIDE

T2L (Twist 2 Left): Slip next stitch to cn and hold at front, purl next st from left hand needle, then K1tbl from cn.

T2R (Twist 2 Right): Slip next st onto cn and hold at back, K1tbl from left-hand needle, then purl st from cn.

Instructions

Row 1 (right side): *P3, T2L; rep from * to last 2 sts, P2.

Row 2: *K3, T2R, rep from * to last 2 sts, K2.

Repeat Rows 1 and 2 for pattern.

SLIP STITCH RIB

Multiple: 5

Instructions

Row 1: *P2, K1, sl 1, K1; rep from * across.

Row 2 (right side): *P3, K2; rep from * across.

Repeat Rows 1 and 2 for pattern.

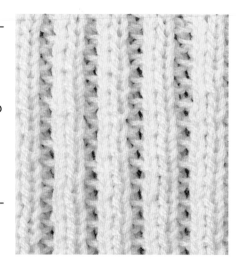

MOSS STITCH RIB

Multiple: 4 + 2

Instructions

Row 1: K1; *K3, P1; repeat from * to last st, K1.

Row 2: K1; *K2, P1, K1; rep from * to last st, K1.

Repeat Rows 1 and 2 for pattern.

HUNTERS RIB

Multiple: 11 + 4

Instructions ───────────

Row 1 (right side): *P4, (K1tbl, P1) 3 times, K1tbl; rep from * across to last 4 sts, P4.

Row 2: *K4, P1, (K1tbl, P1) 3 times; rep from * across to last 4 sts, K4.

Repeat Rows 1 and 2 for pattern.

OPENWORK RIB

Multiple: 4 + 2

Instructions ─────────

Row 1(right side): K1; *K3, P1; rep from * to last st, K1.

Row 2: K1; *K1, P3; rep from * to last st, K1.

Row 3: K1; *YO, sl 1, K2tog, PSSO, YO, P1; rep from * to last st, K1.

Row 4: *K1; *K1, P3; rep from * to last st, K1.

Repeat Rows 1 through 4 for pattern.

BAMBOO RIB

Multiple: 2

Instructions ─────────

Row 1: K1; *YO, K2, pass YO over K2 and drop from needle; rep from * across to last st, K1.

Row 2: K1, purl to last st, K1.

Repeat Rows 1 and 2 for pattern.

PILLAR RIB

Multiple: 4 + 1

STITCH GUIDE

TKS (Triple Knot Stitch):
P3tog, leaving the three purl sts on the left-hand needle and transferring the new stitch onto the right needle, wyib, knit the three purled sts tog again, transferring new stitch onto right needle, then wyif purl the same 3 sts tog, dropping them off left-hand needle.

wyib: with yarn in back

wyif: with yarn in front

Instructions

Row 1 (wrong side): K1; *TKS, K1; rep from * across.

Row 2 (right side): Purl across.

Repeat Rows 1 and 2 for pattern.

MOCK CABLE RIB

Multiple: 7 + 2

Instructions ————

Row 1: K1; *P4, K3; rep from * across to last st, K1.

Row 2: K1; *P3, K4; rep from * across to last st, K1.

Row 3: K1; *P4, sl 1, K2, YO, PSSO (over K2 and YO); rep from * across to last st, K1.

Row 4: K1; *P3, K4; rep from * across to last st, K1.

Repeat Rows 1 through 4 for pattern.

TWEED STITCH RIB

Multiple: 6 + 2

Note: *Slip sts as if to purl.*

Instructions

Row 1 (right side): K1; *P3, sl 1, wyib K1, wyif sl 1; rep from * to last st, K1.

Row 2: K1; *P3, K3; rep from * to last st, K1.

Row 3: K1; *P3, K1, wyif sl 1, wyib K1; rep from * to last st, K1.

Row 4: K1; *P3, K3; rep from * to last st, K1.

Repeat Rows 1 through 4 for pattern.

Embossed Stitches

SEA FOAM

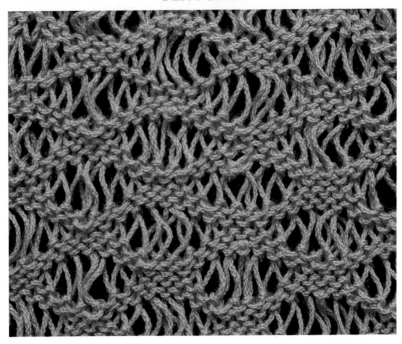

Multiple: 10 + 6

Instructions ————

Row 1: Knit.

Row 2: Knit.

Row 3 (right side): K6; *(YO) twice, K1, (YO) 3 times, K1, (YO) 4 times, K1, (YO) 3 times, K1, (YO) twice, K6; rep from * across,

Row 4: Knit across, dropping all YOs off needle.

Row 5: Knit.

Row 6: Knit.

Row 7: K1; *(YO) twice , K1, (YO) 3 times, K1, (YO) 4 times, K1, (YO) 3 times, K1, (YO) twice, K6; rep from * across, ending last rep with K1 instead of K6.

Row 8: Knit across, dropping all YOs off needle

Repeat Rows 1 through 8 for pattern, ending by working Row 2 or 6.

YO-YO'S

Multiple: 8 + 4

Note: *Slip all stitches as if to purl.*

STITCH GUIDE

Wyif: with yarn in front

Wyib: with yarn in back

Instructions ─────

Row 1 (right side): Knit.

Row 2: Purl.

Rows 3, 5 and 7: P1, wyib, sl 2, wyif, *P6, wyib, sl 2, wyif; rep from * to last st, P1.

Rows 4, 6 and 8: K1, wyif, sl 2, wyib, *K6, wyif, sl 2, wyib; rep from * to last st, K1.

Row 9: Knit across.

Row 10: Purl across.

Rows 11, 13 and 15: P5, wyib, sl 2, wyif; *P6, wyib, sl 2, wyif; rep from * to last 5 sts, P5.

Rows 12, 14 and 16: K5, wyif, sl 2 wyib; *K6, wyif, sl 2, wyib; rep from * to last 5 sts, K5.

Repeat Rows 1 through 16 for pattern, ending by working Row 2 or 10.

FLORETTES

Multiple: 8 sts

STITCH GUIDE

BB (Bobble): (K1, YO, K1) in next st, turn, P3, turn, K3, turn, P2tog, P1, turn, sl 1, K1, PSSO.

Instructions ———————

Row 1 (right side): *P3, K1, P4; rep from * across.

Rows 2, 4 and 6: *K4, P1, K3; rep from * across.

Row 3: *P3, K1, P4; rep from * across.

Row 5: *P2, BB, K1, BB, P3; rep from * across.

Row 7: P3, BB, P4; rep from * across.

Row 8: Knit across.

Rows 9 and 11: P7; *K1, P7; rep from * across to last st, P1.

Rows 10, 12 and 14: K8; *P1, K7; rep from * across.

Row 11: P7; *K1, P7; rep from * across to last st, P1.

Row 13: P6; *BB, K1, BB, P5; rep from * across to last 2 sts, P2.

Row 15: P7; *BB, P7; rep from * across to last st, P1.

Row 16: Knit across.

Repeat Rows 1 through 16 for pattern, ending by working Rows 1 through 4.

CLAM SHELL

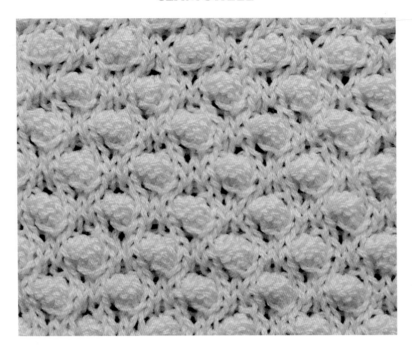

Multiple: 4 + 1

STITCH GUIDE

Shell: [(P1, YO) twice, P1 in next st]

Instructions ——————

Row 1 (wrong side): K2; *Shell in next st, K3; rep from * across, ending last repeat with K2.

Row 2: P2; *K5, P3; rep from * across, ending last rep with P2.

Row 3: K2; *P5, K3; rep from * across, ending last rep with K2.

Row 4: P2; *K5tog tbl, P3; rep from * aross, ending last rep with P2.

Row 5: K4; *Shell in next st, K3; rep from * across to last st, K1.

Row 6: P4; *K5, P3; rep from * across, to last st, P1.

Row 7: K4; *P5, K3; rep from * across to last st, K1.

Row 8: P4; *K5tog tbl, P3; rep from * across to last st, P1.

Repeat Rows 1 through 8 for pattern.

ROSEBUDS

Multiple: 8 + 2

Note: *This stitch uses a cable needle (cn).*

Instructions

Row 1 (wrong side): K1; *K3, P2, K3; rep from * across to last st, K1.

Row 2: K1; *P3, sl next st to cn and hold at front, K1, (YO) 5 times, K1 from cn, P3; rep from * across to last st, K1.

Row 3: K1; *K3, P1, (K1 tbl) 5 times, P1, K3; rep from * across to last st, K1.

Row 4: K1; *P3, (K1, YO) 6 times, K1, P3; rep from * across to last st, K1.

Row 5: K1; *K3, P13, K3; rep from * across to last st, K1.

Row 6: K1; *P3, K13, P3; rep from * across to last st, K1.

Row 7: K1; *K3, P2tog, P9, P2tog tbl, K3; rep from * across to last st, K1.

Row 8: K1; *P3, sl 1, K1, PSSO, K7, K2tog, P3; rep from * across to last st, K1.

Row 9: K1; *K3, P2tog, P5, P2tog tbl, K3; rep from * across to last st, K1.

Row 10: K1; *P3, sl 1, K1, PSSO, K3, K2tog, P3; rep from * across to last st, K1.

Row 11: K1; *K3, P2tog, P1, P2tog tbl, K3; rep from * across to last st, K1.

Row 12: K1; *P3, sl 1, K1, PSSO, K1, P3; rep from * across to last st, K1.

Rep Rows 1 through 12 for pattern.

CLUSTERS

Multiple: 6 + 5

Note: *This stitch uses a cable needle (cn).*

STITCH GUIDE

CL (Cluster): Knit next 3 sts, transfer sts onto cn and wrap yarn 6 times around needle, starting by wrapping around right side; return sts to right-hand needle.

Note: *Be careful that the wraps do not cover a previous wrap but lie in the space above the wrap.*

Instructions

Row 1: Purl across.

Row 2 (right side): Knit across.

Row 3: Purl across.

Row 4: K4; *CL, K3; rep from * across, ending with K1.

Row 5: Purl across.

Row 6: Knit across.

Row 7: Purl across.

Row 8: K1; *CL, K3; rep from * across, endling with CL, K1.

Repeat Rows 1 through 8 for pattern, ending by working Row 1.

ART DECO

Multiple: 13 + 2

STITCH GUIDE

BB (Bobble): In next st, work (K1, P1) twice; turn, P4. Pass 2nd, 3rd and 4th sts one at a time over first st, turn. Knit into back of this st.

Instructions ─────────

Row 1(right side): K1; *P4, K5, P4; rep from * to last st, K1.

Row 2: P1; *K4, P5, K4; rep from * to last st, P1.

Row 3: K1; *P3, K2tog, K1, (YO, K1) twice; K2tog tbl, P3; rep from * to last st, K1.

Row 4: P1; *K3, P7, K3; rep from * to last st, P1.

Row 5: K1; *P2, K2tog, K1, YO, K3, YO, K1, K2tog tbl, P2; rep from * to last st, K1.

Row 6: P1; *K2, P9, K2; rep from * to last st, P1.

Row 7: K1; *P1, K2tog, K1, YO, K5, YO, K1, K2tog tbl, P1; rep from * to last st, K1.

Row 8: P1; *K1, P11, K1; rep from * to last st, P1.

Row 9: K1; *K2tog, K1, YO, K3, BB, K3, YO, K1, K2tog tbl; rep from * to last st, K1.

Row 10: Purl across.

Repeat Rows 1 through 10 for pattern.

ALL-OVER BOBBLES

Multiple: 10+ 2

STITCH GUIDE

BB (Bobble): [(K1, P1) twice, K1 in same st), turn, P5, turn, K3, K2tog, pass 3 sts, one at a time, over K2tog.

Instructions

Row 1: Knit across

Row 2 and all even-numbered rows: K1, purl to last st, K1.

Row 3: Knit across.

Row 5: K1; *K2, YO, SSK, K6; rep from * to last st, K1.

Row 7: K1; *K2tog, YO, K1, YO, SSK, K5; rep from * to last st, K1.

Row 9: K1; *K2, BB, K7; rep from * to last st, K1.

Row 11: Knit across.

Row 13: Knit across.

Row 15: K1; *K7, YO, SSK, K1; rep from * to last st, K1.

Row 17: K1; *K5, K2tog, YO, K1, YO, SSK; rep from * to last st, K1.

Row 19: K1; *K7, BB, K2; rep from * to last st, K1.

Row 20: K1, purl to last st, K1.

Repeat Rows 1 through 20 for pattern.

BELLS

Multiple: 6 + 5

Instructions

Row 1 (right side): P2; *K1, P5; rep from * to last 3 sts, K1, P2.

Row 2: K2; *P1, K5; rep from * to last 3 sts, P1, K2.

Row 3: P5; *YO, K1, YO, P5; rep from * across.

Rows 4, 6 and 8: K5; *P3, K5; rep from * across.

Rows 5 and 7: P5; *K3, P5; rep from * across.

Row 9: P5; *sl 1, K2tog, PSSO, P5; rep from * across.

Rows 10 and 12: K5; *P1, K5; rep from * across.

Row 11: P5; *K1, P5; rep from * across.

Row 13: P2; *YO, K1, YO, P5; rep from * to last 3 sts, YO, K1, YO, P2.

Rows 14, 16 and 18: K2; *P3, K5; rep from * to last 5 sts, P3, K2.

Row 15: P2, *K3, P5; rep from * to last 5 sts, K3, P2.

Row 17: P2, *K3, P5; rep from * to last 5 sts, K3, P2.

Row 19: P2; *sl 1, K2tog, PSSO, P5; rep from * to last 5 sts, sl 1, K2tog, PSSO, P2.

Row 20: K2; *P1, K5; rep from * to last 3 sts, P1, K2.

Repeat Rows 1 through 20 for pattern.

GARTER STITCH BOBBLES

Multiple: 6 + 5

BB (Bobble): [(K1, P1) twice, K1], turn; P5, turn; K5, turn; K2tog, K1, K2tog, turn; sl 1, K2tog, PSSO

Instructions

Rows 1 through 4: Knit.

Row 5: K5; *BB, K5; rep from * across.

Row 6 through 10: Knit.

Row 11: K2; *BB, K5; rep from *, ending last rep wth K2.

Row 12: Knit.

Repeat Rows 1 through 12 for pattern.

BRAMBLE STITCH

Multiple: 4

BB (Bobble): (K1, P1, K1) into same stitch

Instructions

Row 1 (wrong side): K2; *BB, P3tog; rep from * across to last 2 sts, K2.

Row 2: Purl across.

Row 3: K2; *P3tog, BB; rep from * across to last 2 sts, K2.

Row 4: Purl across.

Repeat Rows 1 through 4 for pattern.

CANTERBURY BELLS

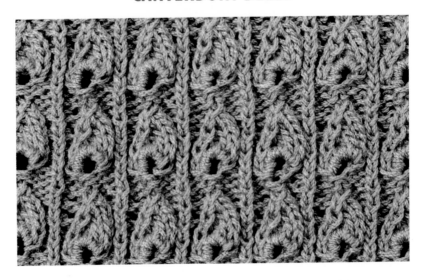

Multiple: 6 + 2

STITCH GUIDE ───────────

INC: Knit into front, then back of next st 3 times, then knit into front: 7 sts made in one st.

Instructions

Row 1 (right side): K1; *P2, K1tbl, P2, INC; rep from * across to last st, K1.

Row 2: K1; *P7, K2, P1, K2; rep from * across to last st, K1.

Row 3: K1, *P2, K1tbl, P2, K5, K2tog; rep from * across to last st, K1.

Row 4: K1; *P2tog, P4, K2, P1, K2; rep from * across to last st, K1.

Row 5: K1; *P2, K1tbl, P2, K3, K2tog; rep from * across to last st, K1.

Row 6: K1; *P2tog, P2, K2, P1, K2; rep from * across to last st, K1.

Row 7: K1; *P2, K1tbl, P2, K1, K2tog; rep from * across to last st, K1.

Row 8: K1; *P2tog, K2, P1, K2; rep from * across to last st, K1.

Row 9: K1; *P2, K1tbl, P3; rep from * across to last st, K1.

Row 10: K1; *K3, P1, K2; rep from * across to last st, K1.

Repeat Rows 1 through 10 for pattern.

SEA SHELLS

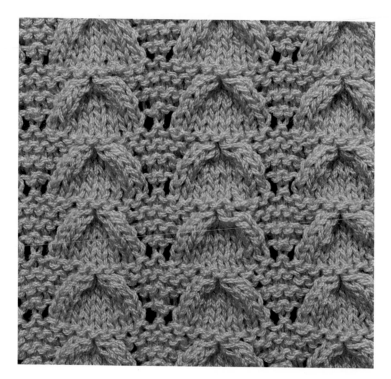

Multiple: 9 + 3

Instructions ───────

Row 1 (right side): K2; *YO, K8, YO, K1; rep from * across to last st, K1.

Row 2: K3; *P8, K3; rep from * across.

Row 3: K3, *YO, K8, YO, K3; rep from * across.

Row 4: K4; *P8, K5; rep from * across, ending last rep with K4.

Row 5: K4; *YO, K8, YO, K5; rep from * across, ending last rep with K4.

Row 6: K5; *P8, K7; rep from * across, ending last rep with K5.

Row 7: K5; *K4tog tbl, K4tog, K7; rep from * across, ending last rep with K5.

Row 8: Knit across.

Repeat Rows 1 through 8 for pattern.

TEARDROPS

Multiple: 6 + 2

Instructions

Row 1 (right side): P2; *M4, P2, K1, P2; rep from * across.

Row 2: *K2, P1, K2, [K1, (YO twice)] 4 times, rep from * to last 2 sts, K2.

Rows 3 and 5: P2; *letting extra loops drop K4, P2, K1, P2; rep from * across.

Row 4: *K2, P1, K2, [K1, (YO twice] 4 times, rep from * to last 2 sts, K2.

Row 6: *K2, P1, K2, P4tog; rep from * across to last 2 sts, K2.

Row 7: P2; *K1, P2, M4, P2 rep from * across.

Rows 8 and 10: *K2, [K1, (YO twice)] 4 times, K2, P1; rep from * across to last 2 sts, K2.

Rows 9 and 11: P2; *K1, P2, letting extra loops drop K4, P2; rep from * across.

Row 12: *K2, P4tog, K2, P1; rep from * across to last 2 sts, K2.

WISHBONES

Multiple: 12 + 4

STITCH GUIDE

wyif: with yarn in front of needle

wyib: with yarn in back of needle

Note: *This pattern uses a cable needle (cn).*

Instructions ───────

Row 1 (right side): P4; *K2, P4; rep from * across.

Row 2: K4; *P2, K4; rep from * across.

Row 3: P4; *K2, P4; rep from * across.

Row 4: K4; *P2, K4; rep from * across.

Row 5: P4; *K2, P4; rep from * across.

Row 6: K4; *wyif sl 2 as to purl, wyib K4; rep from * across.

Row 7: P4; *slip 2 to cn and leave at front, P2, YO, K2tog tbl from cn, sl 2 to cn and leave at back of work, K2tog, YO, P2 from cn, P4; rep from * across.

Row 8: K4; *P2, K1tbl, P2, K1tbl, P2, K4; rep from * across.

Repeat Rows 1 through 8 for pattern.

DOTS AND DASHES

Mutiple: 3 + 2

STITCH GUIDE

M3 (make 3 sts): K1tbl, K1, K1tbl in stitch

Instructions

Row 1 (right side): *P2, K1; rep from * across to last 2 sts, P2.

Row 2: K2; *P1, K2; rep from * across.

Row 3: *P2, K1; rep from * across to last 2 sts, P2.

Row 4: K2; *P1, K2; rep from * across.

Row 5: *P2, K1; rep from * across to last 2 sts, P2.

Row 6: K2; *P1, K2; rep from * across.

Row 7: *P2, M3; rep from * to last 2 sts, P2.

Row 8: K2; *P3, K2; rep from * across.

Row 9: *P2, K3; rep from * to last 2 sts, P2.

Row 10: K2; *P3, K2; rep from * across.

Row 11: *P2, sl 1, K2tog, PSSO; rep from * across to last 2 sts, P2.

Repeat Rows 2 through 11 for pattern, ending by working Row 6.

TRELLIS STITCH

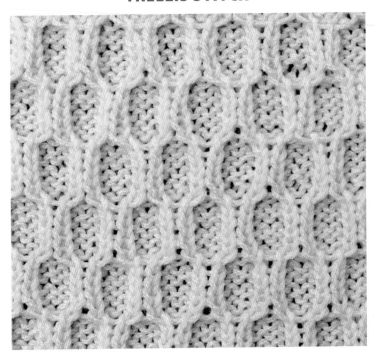

Multiple: 6 + 2

Note: *This stitch uses a cable needle (cn).*

Instructions

Rows 1 and 3 (right side): K1; *P2, K2, P2; rep from * across to last st, K1.

Rows 2 and 4: K1; *K2, P2, K2; rep from * across to last st, K1.

Row 5: K1; *sl 2 sts to cn and hold at back, K1, P2 from cn, sl 1 to cn and hold at front, P2, K1 from cn; rep from * across to last st, K1.

Rows 6, 8 and 10: K1; *P1, K4, P1; rep from * to last st, K1.

Rows 7 and 9: K1; *K1, P4, K1; rep from * across to last st, K1.

Row 11: K1; *sl 1 st to cn and hold at front, P2, K1 from cn; sl 2 sts to cn and hold at back, K1, P2 from cn; rep from * across to last st, K1.

Row 12: K1; *K2, P2, K2; rep from * to last st, K1.

Repeat Rows 1 through 12 for pattern.

KNOTS

Multiple: 2

Instructions ————————

Row 1 (right side): K1, purl to last st, K1.

Row 2: K1; *K1, (K1, P1, K1) into next st; rep from * across to last st, K1.

Row 3: K1; *K3, P1; rep from * across to last st, K1.

Row 4: K1; *K1, P3tog; rep from * across to last st, K1.

Row 5: K1, purl to last st, K1.

Row 6: K1; (K1, P1, K1) into next st, K1; rep from * to last st, K1.

Row 7: K1; *P1, K3; rep from * across to last st, K1.

Row 8: K1; *P3tog, K1; rep from * across to last st, K1.

Repeat Rows 1 through 8 for pattern.

MORE BUBBLES

Multiple: 8 + 4

Note: *Slip all stitches as if to purl.*

STITCH GUIDE

Wyif: with yarn in front

Wyib: with yarn in back

Instructions

Row 1 (wrong side): Knit.

Row 2 (right side): Purl.

Rows 3, 5 and 7: P1, wyib, sl 2, wyif, *P6, wyib, sl 2, wyif ; rep from * to last st, P1.

Rows 4, 6 and 8: K1, wyif, sl 2, wyib, *K6, wyif, sl 2, wyib; rep from * to last st, K1.

Row 9: Knit across.

Row 10: Purl across.

Rows 11, 13 and 15: P5, wyib, sl 2, wyif; *P6, wyib, sl 2, wyif; rep from * to last 5 sts, P5.

Rows 12, 14 and 16: K5, wyif, sl 2 wyib; *K6, wyif, sl 2, wyib; rep from * to last 5 sts, K5.

Repeat Rows 1 through 16 for pattern, ending by working Row 2 or 10.

HONEYCOMB

Multiple: 6 + 4

Instructions

Row 1 (wrong side): K1, P2; *M4, P2, K1, P2; rep from * across to last st, K1.

Row 2 (right side): K1; *K2, P1, K2, [K1, (YO twice)] 4 times, rep from * to last 3 sts, K3.

Rows 3 and 5: K1, P2; * letting extra loops drop K4, P2, K1, P2; rep from * across to last st, K1.

Row 4: K1; *K2, P1, K2, [K1, (YO) twice] 4 times, rep from * to last 3 sts, K3.

Row 6: K1; *K2, P1, K2, P4tog; rep from * across to last 3 sts, K3.

Row 7: K1, P2; *K1, P2, M4, P2 rep from * across to last st, K1.

Rows 8 and 10: K1; *K2, [K1, (YO twice)] 4 times, K2, P1; rep from * across to last 3 sts, K3.

Rows 9 and 11: K1, P2; *K1, P2, letting extra loops drop K4, P2; rep from * across to last st, K1.

Row 12: K1; *K2, P4tog, K2, P1; rep from * across to last 3 sts, K3.

Repeat Rows 1 through 12 for pattern.

CHAINS

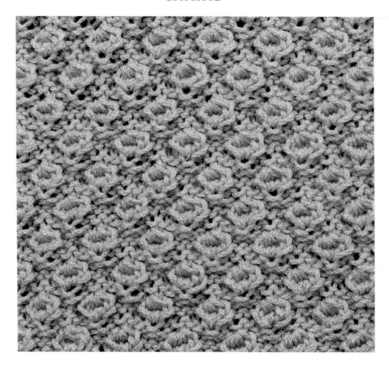

Multiple: 4 + 1

STITCH GUIDE

Shell: [(P1, YO) twice, P1 in next st]

Instructions

Row 1 (right side): K2; *Shell in next st, K3; rep from * across, ending last repeat with K2.

Row 2: P2; *K5, P3; rep from * across, ending last rep with P2.

Row 3: K2; *P5, K3; rep from * across, ending last rep with K2.

Row 4: P2; *K5tog tbl, P3; rep from * aross, ending last rep with P2.

Row 5: K4; *Shell in next st, K3; rep from * across to last st, K1.

Row 6: P4; *K5, P3; rep from * across, to last st, P1.

Row 7: K4; *P5, K3; rep from * across to last st, K1.

Row 8: P4; *K5tog tbl, P3; rep from * across to last st, P1.

Repeat Rows 1 through 8 for pattern.

HOUNDSTOOTH

Multiple: 3 + 2

Note: *Always slip as if to purl*

Two Colors: A and B

Instructions

Row 1 (right side): With Color A, K1; *sl 1, K2; rep from * across to last st, K1.

Row 2: K1, purl to last st, K1.

Row 3 (with Color B): K1, *K2, sl 1; rep from * to last st, K1.

Row 4: K1, purl to last st, K1.

Repeat Rows 1 through 4 for pattern.

Multiple: 6 + 5

Note: *Always slip as if to purl.*

Two Colors: A and B

LADDERS

Instructions

Row 1 (right side): With A, K2, sl 1; *K5, sl 1; rep from * to last 2 sts, K2.

Row 2: With A, P2, sl 1; *P5, sl 1; rep from * to last 2 sts, P2.

Row 3: With B: K5; *sl 1, K5; rep from * to last 5 sts, K5.

Row 4: With B, K5, *wyif sl 1, wyib, K5; rep from * across.

Repeat Rows 1 through 4 for pattern.

CHEVRONS

Multiple: 4 + 2

Three Colors: A, B, and C

Instructions

Row 1: With Color A, K1; purl across to last st, K1.

Row 2 (right side): With B, K1; *K1, sl 3 wyib; rep from * across to last st, K1.

Row 3: With B, K1, P1; *sl 1 wyif, P3; rep from * across, ending with sl 1, P2, K1.

Row 4: With B, knit across.

Row 5: With B, K1, purl across to last st, K1.

Row 6: With C, K1; *K1, sl 3 wyib; rep from * across to last st, K1.

Row 7: With C, K1, P1; *sl 1 wyif, P3; rep from * across, ending with sl 1, P2, K1.

Row 8: With C, knit across.

Row 9: With C, K1, purl across to last st, K1.

Row 10: With A, K1; *K1, sl 3 wyib; rep from * across to last st, K1.

Row 11: With A, K1, P1; *sl 1 wyif, P3; rep from * across, ending with sl 1, P2, K1.

Row 12: With A, knit across.

Row 13: With A, K1, purl across to last st, K1.

Repeat Rows 2 through 13 for pattern.

FLEUR DE LYS

Multiple: 4 + 2

Three Colors: A, B and C

STITCH GUIDE

wyif: with yarn in front

wyib: with yarn in back

Instructions

Row 1 (right side): With A, knit across.

Row 2: With A, purl across.

Row 3: With B, K1; *K3, sl 1; rep from * across to last st, K1.

Row 4: With B, P1; *wyif, sl 1, P3; rep from * to last st, P1.

Row 5: With C, K2; *sl 1, K3; rep from * across.

Row 6: With C, P3; *wyif, sl 1, P3; rep from * to last 3 sts, sl 1, P2.

Row 7: With A, K1; *K3, sl 1; rep from * across to last st, K1.

Row 8: With A, P1; *wyif, sl 1, P3; rep from * to last st, P1.

Row 9: With B, K2; *sl 1, K3; rep from * across.

Row 10: With B, P3; *wyif, sl 1, P3; rep from * to last 3 sts, sl 1, P2.

Row 11: With C, K1; *K3, sl 1; rep from * across to last st, K1.

Row 12: With C, P1; *wyif, sl 1, P3; rep from * to last st, P1.

Row 13: With A, K2; *sl 1, K3; rep from * across.

Row 14: With A, P3; *wyif, sl 1, P3; rep from * to last 3 sts, sl 1, P2.

Repeat Rows 3 through 14 for pattern.

BALLOONS

Multiple: 8 + 4

Three Colors: A, B and C

Note: *Slip all sts as if to purl.*

Instructions ─────────

Row 1 (right side): With A, knit across.

Row 2: With A, knit across. Cut Color A; attach Color B.

Rows 3, 5 and 7: With B, K1, sl 2; *K6, sl 2; rep from * to last st, K1.

Rows 4, 6 and 8: With B, P1, sl 2; *P6, sl 2; rep from * to last st, P1.

Rows 9 and 10: With A, knit across.

Rows 11, 13 and 15: With C, K5, sl 2; *K6, sl 2; rep from * to last 5 sts, K5.

Rows 12, 14 and 16: With C, P5, sl 2; *P6, sl 2; rep from * to last 5 sts, P5.

Repeat Rows 1 through 16 for pattern, ending by working Row 2.

STAR STITCH

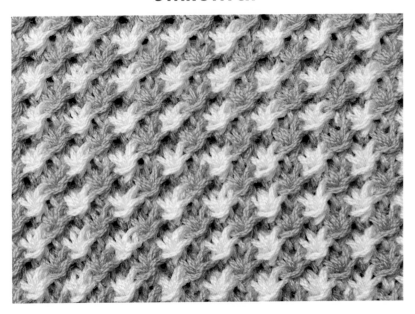

Multiple: 4 + 1

Two Colors: A and B

STITCH GUIDE

MS (Make Star): P3tog, leaving sts on left-hand needle, YO, then purl same 3 sts tog again.

Instructions

Row 1 (right side): With Color A, knit across.

Row 2: With Color A, P1, *MS, P1; rep from * across.

Row 3: With Color B, knit across.

Row 4: With Color B: P3, MS; *P1, MS; rep from * to last 3 sts, P3.

Repeat Rows 1 through 4 for pattern, ending by working a Row 1.

PLAITED

Multiple 4 + 2

Two colors: A and B
Note: *This pattern uses a cable needle (cn).*

Instructions ——————

Row 1: With A, K3, *K2; with B, K2 with A; rep from * across to last 3 sts, K2 with B, K1 with A.

Rows 2, 6, 10 and 14: With A, K1; *with B, P2; with A, P2; rep from * to last st, with A, K1.

Rows 3, 7 and 11: With A, K1, *sl 2 A sts onto cn and leave at back; with B, K2, then with A, knit sts on cn; rep from * across to last st, with A K1.

Rows 4 , 8 and 12: With A, K1, *P2 with A; with B, P2; rep from * to last st; with A, K1.

Rows 5, 9 and 13: With A, K3, *sl 2 A sts onto cn and leave at front; with B, K2; then with A, knit sts from cn; rep from * across to last 3 sts, with B, K2 ; with A, K1.

Repeat Rows 1 through 14 for pattern.

BI-COLOR KNIT

Multiple: 6 + 2

Two Colors: A and B

Instructions

Row 1 (right side): With Color A, knit across.

Row 2: With A, K1, purl to last st, K1.

Rows 3 and 5: With Color B, K4; *wyib sl 1, K5; rep across to last 4 sts, wyib sl 1, K3.

Rows 4 and 6: With B, K3; *wyif sl 1, wyib K5; rep from * across to last 5 sts, wyif sl 1, wyib K4.

Row 7: With A, knit across.

Row 8: With A, K1, purl to last st, K1.

Rows 9 and 11: With B, K1; *wyib sl 1, K5; rep from * across to last st, K1.

Rows 10 and 12: With B, K1; *K5, wyif sl 1, wyib; rep from * across to last 2 sts, wyif sl 1, wyib K1.

Repeat Rows 1 through 12 for pattern, ending by working Rows 1 and 2.

LOOP DE LOOP

Multiple: 2 + 3

Two colors: A and B

Note: *Slip all sts as if to purl.*

Instructions ───────

Row 1 (right side): With A, knit across.

Row 2: With A, K1, purl across to last st, K1.

Row 3: With B, K2; *sl 1, K1; rep from * across to last st, K1.

Row 4: With B, K2; *sl 1, K1; rep from * across to last st, K1.

Row 5: With B, knit across.

Row 6: With B, K1, purl across to last st, K1.

Row 7: With A, K3, sl 1; *K1, sl 1; rep from * to last 3 sts, K3.

Row 8: With A, K1, P1, K1; *sl 1, K1; rep from * to last 2 sts, P1, K1.

Repeat Rows 1 through 8 for pattern.

───────

CHECK

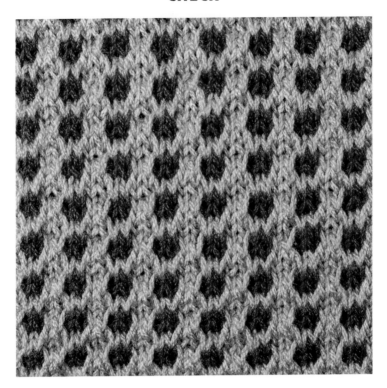

Multiple: 4 + 2

Three Colors: A, B and C

Note: *Slip all sts as if to purl.*

Instructions ———————

Row 1 (wrong side): With A, K1, purl across to last st, K1.

Row 2: With B, K4, sl 2; *K2, sl 2; rep from * to last 4 sts, K4.

Row 3: With B, K1, P3, sl 2; *P2, sl 2; rep from * to last 4 sts, P3, K1.

Row 4: With A, knit across.

Row 5: With C, K1, P1, sl 2; *P2, sl 2; rep from * to last 2 sts, P1, K1.

Row 6: With C, K2, sl 2; *K2, sl 2; rep from * to last 2 sts, K2.

Repeat Rows 1 through 6 for pattern.

SMOCKING

Multiple: 6 + 5

Two colors: A and B

Note: *Always slip as if to purl.*

Instructions

Row 1 (right side): With A, knit across.

Row 2 (wrong side): With A, P4; * wyib sl 3, P3; rep from * across, ending last rep with P1.

Rows 3, 5, 9 and 11: With B, knit across.

Rows 4 and 6: With B, P4; * wyib sl 3, P3; rep from * to last st, P1.

Row 7: With A, K5; *KS, K5; rep from * across.

Row 8: With A, P1; * wyib sl 3, P3; rep from * across ending last rep with P1.

Rows 10 and 12: With B, P1; * wyib sl 3, P3; rep from * across ending last rep with P1.

Row 13: With A, K2; *KS, K5; rep from * across, ending last rep with K2.

Repeat Rows 2 through 13 for pattern.

TWO-COLOR CABLE

Multiple: 12 + 4

Two Colors: A and B

Note: *This uses a cable needle (cn) and bobbins for Color B.*

Instructions

Rows 1, 3 and 7: With A, K1, *K2, P2; with B K2; with A K2; with B K2; with A P2; rep from * across to last 3 sts, with A K3.

Rows 2, 4, 6 and 8: With A, K1, P2, *K2; with B P2; with A P2; with B P2; with A K2, P2; rep from * to last st, with A K1.

Row 5: With A K1, * K2, P2; sl 4 sts to cn at hold at front of work; with B K2; sl 2 color A from cn onto left needle and knit them with A; sl 2 color B from cn onto left needle and knit them with color B; with A P2; rep from * across to last 3 sts, with A K3.

Repeat Rows 1 through 8 for pattern.

TWO-COLOR CROSSED STITCHES

Multiple: 2 + 3

Two Colors: A and B

Note: *Always slip as if to purl.*

Instructions

Row 1: With Color A: K1; *sl 1, K1, YO, P2SSO, rep from * across to last 2 sts, K2.

Row 2: With Color A: K1, purl to last st, K1.

Row 3: With Color B, K2; *sl 1, K1, YO, P2SSO; rep from * across to last st, K1.

Row 4: With Color B, K1, purl to last st, K1.

Repeat Rows 1 through 4 for pattern.

3-COLOR LADDER

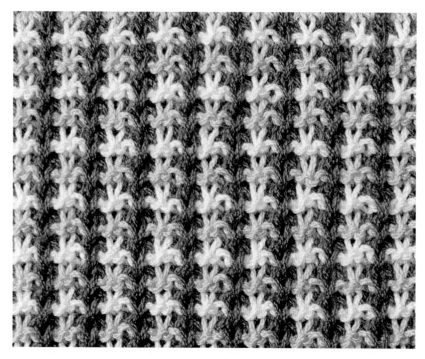

Multiple: 4 + 3

Three Colors: A, B and C

Note: *Slip all sts as if to purl.*

Instructions

Row 1: With A, purl.

Row 2 (right side): With B, K3; *sl 1, K3; rep from * across.

Row 3: With B, K3; *wyif sl 1, wyib K3; rep from * across.

Row 4: With A, K1, sl 1; *K3, sl 1; rep from * to last st, K1.

Row 5: With A, P1, sl 1; *P3, sl 1; rep from * to last st, P1.

Row 6: With C, K3; *sl 1, K3; rep from * across.

Row 7: With C, K3; *wyif sl 1, wyib K3; rep from * across.

Row 8: With A, K1, sl 1; *K3, sl 1; rep from * to last st, K1.

Row 9: With A, P1, sl 1; *P3, sl 1; rep from * to last st, P1.

Repeat Rows 2 through 9 for pattern.

COLOR LOOPS

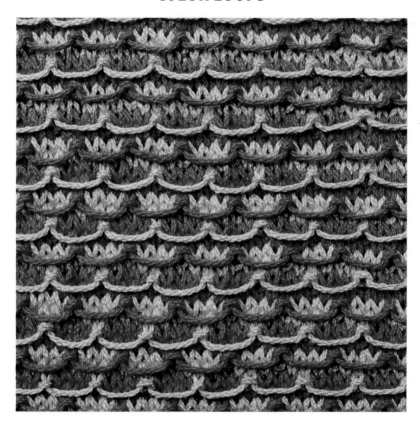

Multiple: 4 + 1

Two Colors: A and B

Note: *Always slip as if to purl.*

Instructions

Row 1: With A, knit across.

Row 2: With A, purl across.

Row 3: With B, K1; * sl 3, K1; rep from * across.

Row 4: With B, K1; * sl 3, K1; rep from * across.

Row 5: With B, knit across.

Row 6: With B, purl across.

Row 7: With A, K3, sl 3; *K1, sl 3; rep from * to last 3 sts, K3.

Row 8: With A, P2, K1; * sl 3, K1; rep from * to last 2 sts, P2.

Repeat Rows 1 through 8 for pattern.

COLORFUL MOSS

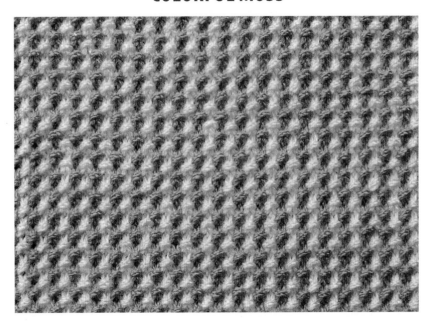

Multiple: 2

Two Colors: A and B

Note: *Always slip as if to purl.*

Instructions

Row 1: With Color A, K1; *K1, sl 1; rep from * across to last st, K1.

Row 2: With Color A, K1; *wyif sl 1, K1; rep from * across to last st, K1.

Row 3: With Color B, K1; *sl 1, K1; rep from * across to last st, K1.

Row 4: With Color B, K1; *K1, wyif sl 1; rep from * across to last st, K1.

Repeat Rows 1 through 4 for pattern.

PLAID

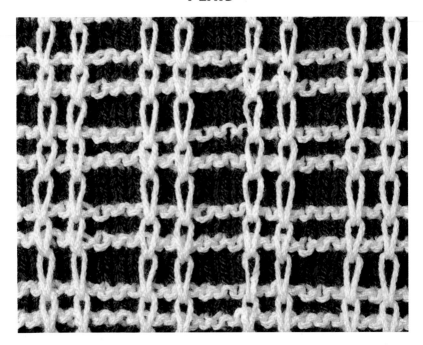

Multiple: 8 + 2

Two Colors: A and B

Instructions ───────

Rows 1 and 5 (right side): With B, K1; *KW, K2, KW, K4; rep from * across, ending row with K1.

Rows 2 and 6: With B, K1; *K4, wyif sl 1 dropping extra wraps off needle, K2, wyif sl 1 dropping extra wraps off needle, rep from * across, ending row with K1.

Rows 3, 7 and 9: With A, K1; *wyib sl 1, K2, wyib sl 1, K4; rep from * across, ending row with K1.

Rows 4, 8 and 10: With A, K1; *P4, wyif sl 1, P2, wyif sl 1; rep from * across, ending row with K1.

Repeat Rows 1 through 10 for pattern.

───────────────────

TRI-COLOR

Multiple: 2

Three colors: A, B and C

Note: Always slip as if to purl.

Instructions ———————

Row 1 (right side): With A, K1; *wyif sl 1, wyib K1; rep from * across to last st, K1.

Row 2: With B, K1; *wyib sl 1, wyif P1; rep from * across to last st, wyib K1.

Row 3: With C, K1; *wyif sl 1, wyib K1; rep from * across to last st, K1.

Row 4: With A, K1; *wyib sl 1, wyif P1; rep from * across to last st, K1.

Row 5: With B, K1; *wyif sl 1, wyib K1; rep from * across to last st, K1.

Row 6: With C, K1; *wyib sl 1, wyif P1; rep from * across to last st, K1.

Repeat Rows 1 through 6 for pattern.

Eyelets and Cables

LACE DIAMONDS

Multiple: 10 + 2

Instructions —————

Row 1 (right side): K1; *YO, sl 1, K1, PSSO, K1, K2tog, (YO) twice, sl 1, K1, PSSO, K1, K2tog, YO; rep from * to last st, K1.

Row 2 and all even rows: K1, purl to last st, K1.

Note: *Purl into first YO and Ptbl though second YO.*

Row 3: K1; *K2tog, YO, K6, YO, sl 1, K1, PSSO; rep from * to last st, K1.

Row 5: K1; *K1, K2tog, YO, K4, YO, sl 1, K1, PSSO, K1; rep from * to last st, K1.

Row 7: K1; *K2, K2tog, YO, K2, YO, sl 1, K1, PSSO, K2; rep from * to last st, K1.

Row 9: K1; *YO, sl 1, K1, PSSO, K1, K2tog, (YO) twice, sl 1, K1, PSSO, K1, K2tog, YO; rep from * to last st, K1.

Row 11: K1, *K3, YO, sl 1, K1, PSSO, K2tog, YO, K3; rep from * across to last st, K1.

Row 13: K1; *K2, YO, sl 1, K1, PSSO, K2, K2tog, YO, K2; rep from * across to last st, K1.

Row 15: K1; *K1, YO, sl 1, K1, PSSO, K4, K2tog, YO, K1; rep from * across to last st, K1.

Row 16: K1, purl to last st, K1.

Repeat Rows 1 through 16 for pattern.

LITTLE FLOWERS

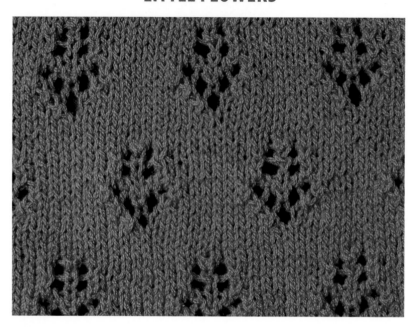

Multiple: 12 + 7

Instructions

Row 1 (right side): K3; *YO, K2tog, K10; rep from * across to last 4 sts, YO, K2tog, K2.

Row 2 and all even rows: K1, purl to last st, K1.

Rows 3, 7 and 9: K4; *YO, K2tog, K7, sl 1, K1, PSSO, YO, K1; rep from * to last 3 sts, K3.

Row 5: K4; *K1, YO, K2tog, K5, sl 1, K1, PSSO, YO, K2; rep from * to last 3 sts, K3.

Rows 11 and 13: Knit across.

Row 15: K9; *YO, K2tog, K10; rep from * to last 10 sts, YO, K2tog, K8.

Rows 17, 21 and 23: K7; *sl 1, K1, PSSO, YO, K1, YO, K2tog, K7; rep from * across.

Row 19: K6; *sl 1, K1, PSSO, YO, K3, YO, K2tog, K5; rep from * across to last st, K1.

Rows 25 and 27: Knit across.

Row 28: K1, purl to last st, K1.

Repeat Rows 1 through 28 for pattern.

TRELLIS

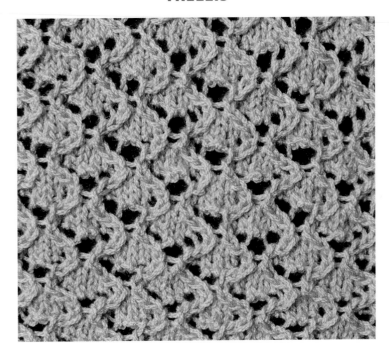

Multiple 7 + 2

Instructions

Row 1 (right side): K1; *K2, K2tog, YO, K3; rep from * across to last st, K1.

Row 2: K1; *P1, P2tog tbl, YO, P1, YO, P2tog, P1; rep from * across to last st, K1.

Row 3: K1; *K2tog, YO, K3, YO, sl 1, K1, PSSO; rep from * across to last st, K1.

Row 4: K1, purl to last st, K1.

Row 5: K1; *YO, sl 1, K1, PSSO, K5; rep from * across to last st, K1.

Row 6: K1; *YO, P2tog, P2, P2togtbl, YO, P1; rep from * across to last st, K1.

Row 7: K1: *K2, YO, sl 1, K1 PSSO, K2tog, YO, K1; rep from * across to last st, K1.

Row 8: K1, purl to last st, K1.

Repeat Rows 1 through 8 for pattern.

FEATHER STITCH

Multiple: 7 + 2

Instructions

Row 1 (right side): K1; *P1, P2tog, YO, K1, YO, P2tog, P1; rep from * to last st, K1.

Row 2: K1; purl to last st, K1.

Row 3: Knit across.

Row 4: K1, purl to last st, K1.

Repeat Rows 1 through 4 for pattern.

ARROWS

Multiple 12 + 2

Note: *This pattern uses a cable needle (cn).*

Instructions

Rows 1, 3, 5 and 7 (wrong side): K1, purl to last st, K1.

Row 2: K1; *sl next 3 sts to cn and hold in back, K3, K3 from cn; sl next 3 sts to cn and hold in front, K3, K3 from cn; rep from * to last st, K1.

Rows 4, 6 and 8: Knit across.

Repeat Rows 1 through 8 for pattern.

CELLULAR

Multiple: 4 + 2

Note: *An extra stitch will be the result of Row 1. Row 3 will correct this.*

Instructions ──────

Row 1 (right side): K1, YO, sl 1, K2tog, PSSO, *YO, K1, YO, sl 1, K2tog, PSSO; rep from * to last 2 sts, (YO, K1) twice.

Row 2: K1; purl to last st, K1.

Row 3: K1, YO, K2tog; *YO, sl 1, K2tog, PSSO, YO, K1; rep from * to last 4 sts, YO, sl 1, K2 tog, PSSO, K1.

Row 4: K1, purl to last st, K1.

Repeat Rows 1 through 4 for pattern.

EYELET STITCH

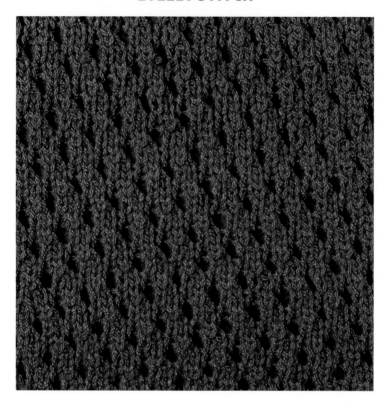

Multiple: 5 + 2

Instructions ─────────

Row 1 (right side): K1; *K3, YO, K2tog; rep from * across to last st, K1.

Row 2 and all even rows: K1, purl to last st, K1.

Row 3: K2; *YO, K2tog, K3; rep from * across.

Row 5: K5; *YO, K2tog, K3; rep from * across to last 2 sts, K2.

Row 7: K3; *YO, K2tog, K3; rep from * across, ending last rep with K2.

Row 9: K1; *YO, K2tog, K3; rep from * to last st, K1.

Row 10: K1, purl to last st, K1.

Repeat Rows 1 through 10 for pattern.

SNOWDROP

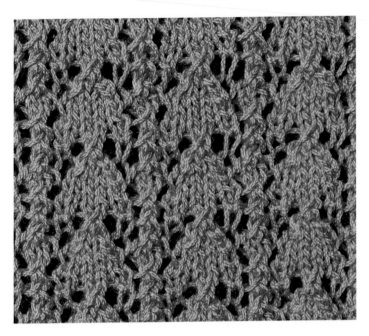

Multiple 8 + 5

STITCH GUIDE

Dbl dec (double decrease): K2togtbl, place stitch on left needle, pass next st over it and then replace it on right needle.

Instructions

Row 1 (right side): K1; *YO, Dbl dec, YO, K5, rep from * across to last 4 sts, YO, Dbl dec, YO, K1.

Row 2 and all even rows: K1, purl to last st, K1.

Row 3: K1; *YO, Dbl dec, YO, K5,: rep from * across to last 4 sts, YO, Dbl dec, YO, K1.

Row 5: K1; *K3, YO, sl 1, K1, PSSO, K1, K2tog, YO; rep from * across to last 4 sts, K4.

Row 7: K1; *YO, dbl dec, YO, K1; rep from * across to last 4 sts, YO, dbl dec, YO, K1.

Row 8: K1, purl to last st, K1.

Repeat Rows 1 through 8 for pattern.

LACE LATTICE

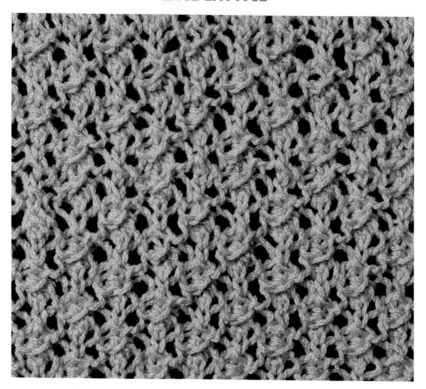

Multiple: 6 + 3

Instructions

Row 1 (right side): K2; *YO, P1, P3tog, P1, YO, K1; rep from * to last st, K1.

Row 2 and all even rows: K1, purl to last st, K1.

Row 3: *K3, YO, sl 1, K2tog, PSSO, YO; rep from * to last 3 sts, K3.

Row 5: K1, P2tog, P1, YO, K1, YO, P1; *P3tog, P1, YO, K1, YO, P1; rep from * to last 3 sts, P2tog, K1.

Row 7: K1, K2tog, YO, K3, YO; *sl 1, K2tog, PSSO, YO, K3, YO; rep from * to last 3 sts, sl 1, K1, PSSO, K1.

Row 8: K1, purl to last st, K1.

Repeat rows 1 through 8 for pattern.

SNOWFLAKE EYELET

Multiple: 8 + 7

Instructions

Row 1 (and all wrong-side rows): K1, purl to last st, K1.

Row 2 (right side): K5; *sl 1, K1, PSSO, YO, K1, YO, K2tog, K3; rep from * across to last 2 sts, K2.

Row 4: K6; *YO, sl 2, K1, P2SSO, YO, K5; rep from * across to last st, K1.

Row 6: K5; *sl 1, K1, PSSO, YO, K1, YO, K2tog, K3; rep from * across to last 2 sts, K2.

Row 8: K1, sl 1, K1, PSSO, YO, K1, YO, K2tog; *K3, sl 1, K1, PSSO, YO, K1, YO, K2tog; rep from * across to last st, K1.

Row 10: K2, *YO, sl 2, K1, P2SSO, YO, K5; rep from * across ending last rep with K2.

Row 12: K1, sl 1, K1, PSSO, YO, K1, YO, K2tog; *K3, sl 1, K1, PSSO, YO, K1, YO, K2tog; rep from * across to last st, K1.

Repeat Rows 1 through 12 for pattern, ending by working Row 1.

LACE PYRAMIDS

Multiple 12 + 3

Instructions

Row 1 (and all wrong side rows): K1, purl to last st, K1.

Row 2 (right side): K2; *(K2tog, YO) 5 times, K2; rep from * to last st, K1.

Row 4: K3; *(K2tog, YO) 4 times, K4; rep from * across.

Row 6: K4; *(K2tog, YO) 3 times, K6; rep from * across, ending last rep with K5.

Row 8: *K5, (K2tog, YO) twice, K3; rep from * to last 6 sts, K6.

Row 10: K6; *K2tog, YO, K10; rep from * across, ending last rep with K7.

Row 12: K3, (YO, sl 1, K1, PSSO) twice, *K2, (YO, sl 1, K1, PSSO) 5 times; rep from * across, ending last rep with K2, (YO, sl 1, K1, PSSO) twice, K2.

Row 14: K2, (YO, sl 1, K1, PSSO) twice; *K4 (YO, sl 1, K1, PSSO) 4 times; rep from * across, ending last rep with K4, (YO, sl 1, K1, PSSO) twice, K1.

Row 16: K3, YO, sl 1, K1, PSSO; *K6, (YO, sl 1, K1, PSSO) 3 times; rep from * across, ending last rep with K6, YO, sl 1, K1, PSSO, K2.

Row 18: K2, YO, sl 1, K1, PSSO, *K8, (YO, sl 1, K1, PSSO) twice; rep from * across ending last rep with K8, YO, sl 1, K1, PSSO, K1.

Row 20: K13; *YO, sl 1, K1, PSSO, K10; rep from * to last 2 sts, K2.

Repeat Rows 1 through 20 for pattern, ending by working Row 1.

SAND

Multiple: 12 + 2

Note: *This pattern uses a cable needle (cn).*

Instructions

Row 1 (right side): Knit across.

Rows 2, 4 and 6: K1, purl to last st, K1.

Row 3: K1; *sl next 3 sts on to cn and leave at front of work, K3, K3 from cn, K6; rep from * to last st, K1.

Row 5: Knit across.

Row 7: K1; *K6, sl next 3 sts on to cn and leave at back of work, K3, K3 from cn; rep from * to last st, K1.

Row 8: K1, purl to last st, K1.

Repeat Rows 1 through 8 for pattern.

ALTERNATING CABLES

Multiple: 9 + 5

Note: *This pattern uses a cable needle (cn).*

Instructions

Row 1 (right side): K1; *P3, K6; rep from * to last 4 sts, P3, K1.

Row 2: K1; *K3, P6; rep from * to last 4 sts, K4.

Row 3: K1; *P3, sl next 2 sts on to cn and hold at back of work, K2, K2 sts from cn, K2; rep from * across to last 4 sts, P3, K1.

Row 4: K1; *K3, P6; rep from * to last 4 sts, K4.

Row 5: K1; *P3, K2, sl next 2 sts on to cn and hold at front of work, K2, K2 sts from cn; rep from * to last 4 sts, P3, K1.

Row 6: K1; *K3, P6; rep from * to last 4 sts, K4.

Repeat Rows 3 through 6 for pattern.

LACY CABLE

Multiple: 11 + 9

Note: *This pattern uses a cable needle (cn).*

Instructions

Row 1 and all odd rows: K1, purl to last st, K1.

Row 2 (right side): K2; *YO, sl 1, K1, PSSO, K1, K2tog, YO, K6; rep from * to last 7 sts, YO, sl 1, K1, PSSO, K1, K2tog, YO, K2.

Row 4: K3; *YO, sl 1, K2tog, PSSO, YO, K1, sl next 3 sts to cn and hold at back, K3, then K3 from cn, K1; rep from * to last 6 sts, YO, sl 1, K2tog, PSSO, YO, K3.

Row 6: K2; *YO, sl 1, K1, PSSO, K1, K2tog, YO, K6; rep from * to last 7 sts, YO, sl 1, K1, PSSO, K1, K2tog, YO, K2.

Row 8: K3; *YO, sl 1, K2tog, PSSO, YO, K8; rep from * to last 6 sts, YO, sl 1, K2tog, PSSO, YO, K3.

Repeat Rows 1 through 8 for pattern, ending by working Row 1.

OCTAVIA

Multiple: 20 + 4

Note: *This pattern uses a cable needle (cn).*

Instructions

Row1: K1; *P2, K8; rep from * to last 3 sts, P2, K1.

Row 2 and all even rows: K1; *K2, P8; rep from * to last 3 sts, K3.

Rows 3 and 7 : K1; *P2; sl 4 sts on to cn and hold at front, K4, K4 from cn, P2, K8; rep from * across to last 3 sts, P2, K1.

Rows 5, 9 and 13: K1; *P2, K8; rep from * to last 3 sts, P2, K1.

Rows 11 and 15: K1; *P2, K8, P2, sl 4 sts to cn and hold at front, K4, K4 from cn; rep from * across row to last 3 sts, P2, K1.

Row 16: K1; *K2, P8; rep from * to last 3 sts, P2, K1.

Repeat Rows 1 through 16 for pattern.

INTERLACING CABLE

Multiple: 8 + 6

Note: *This pattern uses a cable needle (cn).*

Instructions

Rows 1, 3, 5, 17 and 19 (right side): K2; *P2, K2; rep from * across.

Rows 2, 4, 6, 16, 18 and 20: P2; *K2, P2; rep from * across.

Row 7: K2, P2, *sl 4 sts on to cn and hold at back, K2, K4 from cn, P2; rep from * to last 2 sts, K2.

Rows 8, 10, 12 and 14: P2, K2; *P6, K2; rep from * across to last 2 sts, P2.

Rows 9, 11 and 13: K2, P2, *K2, K2tog, YO, K2, P2; rep from * across ending last rep with K2.

Row 15: K2, P2; *sl 4 sts to cn and hold at back, K2, (P2, K2) from cn, P2; rep from * across to last 2 sts, K2.

Rows 21: *Sl 2 sts to cn and hold at front, K4, K2 from cn, P2; rep from *across ending last rep with K2 from cn.

Rows 22, 24, 26, 28: *P6, K2; rep from * across ending last rep with P6.

Rows 23, 25 and 27: *K2, K2tog, YO, K2, P2; rep from * across, ending last rep with K2.

Row 29: *Sl 2 sts on to cn and hold at front, K2, P2, K2 sts from cn, P2; rep from * across, ending last rep with K2 from cn.

Row 30: P2; *K2, P2; rep from * across.

Repeat Rows 1 through 30 for pattern.

SHADOW CABLE

Multiple 8 + 2

Note: *This pattern uses a cable needle.*

Instructions

Row 1 and all odd rows: K1, purl to last st, K1.

Row 2 (right side): Knit across.

Row 4: K1; *sl 2 sts to cn and hold at back, K2, K2 from cn, K4; rep from * to last st, K1.

Row 6: Knit across.

Row 8: K1; *K4, sl next 2 sts to cn and hold at front, K2, K2 from cn; rep from * to last st, K1.

Repeat Rows 1 through 8 for pattern, ending by working Row 1.

DIAGONAL WAVE

Multiple: 6+3

Note: *This pattern uses a cable needle.*

Instructions

Row 1 (wrong side): K3; *P3, K3; rep from * across.

Rows 2, 4, 7, 9 and 11: P3; *K3, P3; rep from * across.

Rows 3, 5, 8 and 10: K3; *P3, K3; rep from * across.

Row 6: *Sl 3 sts to cn and hold at back, K3, P3 from cn; rep from * across to last 3 sts, K3.

Row 12: P3, *sl next 3 sts to cn and hold at back, K3, P3 from cn; rep from * across.

Repeat Rows 1 through 12 for pattern.

KISSES

Multiple 12 + 2

Note: *This pattern uses a cable needle (cn).*

Instructions

Row 1 and all odd rows: K1, purl to last st, K1.

Row 2 (right side): Knit across.

Row 4: K1; *sl 2 sts to cn and hold at back, K2, K2 from cn, K4; sl 2 sts to cn and hold in front, K2, K2 from cn; rep from * to last st, K1.

Row 6: Knit across.

Row 8: K3, sl 2 sts to cn and hold in front, K2, K2 from cn; sl 2 sts to cn and hold in back, K2, K2 from cn; *K4, sl 2 sts to cn and hold in front, K2, K2 from cn; sl 2 sts to cn and hold in back, K2, K2 from cn; rep from * to last 3 sts, K3.

Repeat Rows 1 through 8 for pattern.

General Instructions

Abbreviations and Symbols

Knit patterns are written in a special shorthand, which is used so that instructions don't take up too much space. They sometimes seem confusing, but once you learn them, you'll have no trouble following them.

These are Standard Abbreviations

Approx	approximately
BB	bobble
Beg	beginning
BL	back loop
BO	bind off
CL	cluster
Cm	centimeter
Cn	cable needle
Cont	continue
Dbl dec	double decrease
Dec	decrease
FL	front loop
Foll	following
G	grams
Inc	increase(ing)
K	knit
K1B	knit one below
K1tbl	knit one through back loop
K2tog	knit two stitches together
K4tog	knit 4 stitches together
Kn	Knob
KS	Knot stich
Lp(s)	loop(s)
Lpst	loop stitch
LS	Long stitch
M	meter(s)
MB	Mini bobble
M3	make 3 sts in one stitch
M4	make 4 sts in one stitch
M5	make 5 sts in one stitch
Mm	millimeter(s)
Oz	ounces
P	purl
Patt	pattern
P2tog	purl two stitches together
Patt	pattern
PC	Popcorn
PCS	Popcorn stitch
Prev	previous
PS	Puff Stitch
PSKYO	Pass slip stitch over knit stitch and YO
PSSO	pass the slipped stitch over
Ptbl	purl through the back loop
Rem	remain(ing)

Rep	repeat(ing)
Rev	reverse
Rnd	round
Sl	slip
Sl st(s)	slip stitch(es)
Sp(s)	space (s)
SSK	Slip, slip, knit
St(s)	stitch(es)
St st	stockinette stitch
T2L	twist 2 left
T2R	twist 2 right
Tbl	through back loop
TKS	triple knot stitch
Tog	together
Wyib	With yarn in back
Wyif	With yarn in front
YB	yarn in back of needle
Yd(s)	yard (s)
YF	yarn in front of needle
YO	Yarn over the needle
YRN	Yarn around needle

These are Standard Symbols

* An asterisk (or double asterisks**) in a pattern row, indicates a portion of instructions to be used more than once. For instance, "rep from * three times" means that after working the instructions once, you must work them again three times for a total of 4 times in all.

† A dagger (or double daggers ††) indicates that those instructions will be repeated again later in the same row or round.

: The number after a colon tells you the number of stitches you will have when you have completed the row or round.

( ) Parentheses enclose instructions which are to be worked the number of times following the parentheses. For instance, "(K1, P2) 3 times" means that you knit one stitch and then purl two stitches, three times.

Parentheses often set off or clarify a group of stitches to be worked into the same space or stitch.

[ ] Brackets and ( ) parentheses are also used to give you additional information. For instance, "(rem sts are left unworked)"

Knit Terminology

The patterns in this book have been written using the knitting terminology that is used in the United States. Terms which may have different equivalents in other parts of the world are listed below.

United States	International
Gauge	tension
Skip	miss
Yarn over (YO)	yarn forward (yfwd)
Bind off	Cast off